Reflections on Purpose

An Anthology

Compiled by
C. Nathaniel Brown

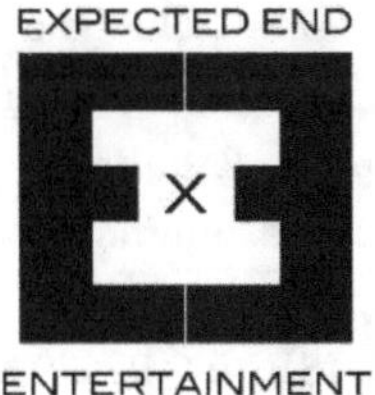

Expected End Entertainment, P.O. Box 1751, Mableton, GA 30126.
ExpectedEndEntertainment@gmail.com
Published by Expected End Entertainment/EX3 Books
ISBN: 0-9968932-9-6
ISBN-13: 978-0-9968932-9-9
Printed in the United States of America

DEDICATION

To everyone who believes in walking in purpose.

CONTENTS

INTRODUCTION

"The two most important days in your life are the day you were born...and the day you find out why." Mark Twain profoundly articulated the importance of our existence and its direct correlation to our purpose and meaning for being here. The sad thing about that is many never take that journey to discovery and many don't care. But for anyone who has ever been impacted by a person walking confidently in their purpose, they understand the magnitude of the why.

Purpose is the reason something is done. It is your why. Purpose is that driving force that keeps you moving forward when you feel the world is pushing you back. It makes sense that when used as a verb, it speaks of intention.

When I was in middle school, I had already decided that I would leave Baltimore to attend college. Yes, I wanted to flee the environment and the conditions that I saw as vices for most in my immediate circle. But more important than running from something, I was running toward something... purpose. I knew from the time I was 4 or 5 that I was different, that I was destined for something other than what I was seeing. Not many supported my choice but not could see the purpose that I saw up ahead. I had to determine that no matter what happened, no matter what anyone said, I had to pursue and fulfill purpose because hundreds or thousands or maybe even millions of people depended on me to live out my purpose.

The writers who have contributed to this anthology are not perfect. Neither am I. But we have accepted the challenge to share about purpose on purpose because we believe in the journey of purpose. Many of us write through our vulnerabilities to help others. Purpose will make you do some things that those operating without purpose will never understand.

I know that my purpose is bigger than me and my circumstances so I have push through to stay on the path of purpose for others. I often share that people are literally dying waiting on you to fulfill your purpose.

So, I admonish you to read these chapters and begin your journey or continue your journey toward purpose. Although you may reap some rewards of this journey, the biggest reward will be witnessing the impact that you will have on others simply by being and doing what you were born to do.

C. Nathaniel Brown

Writer/Publisher

1

ANOTHER CHANCE

KINEH SAM N'GAOJIA

The Whole of Life is about another chance, and while we are alive, till the very end. **THERE IS ALWAYS ANOTHER CHANCE.**" –Jeanette Winterson

This statement could not be any truer pertaining to my life. I am what you would refer to as a survivor. The belief is if you have survived various attempts on your life then you are destined for greatness. On a large scale, God is planning something phenomenal to occur in your life. I, and so many others, believe this to be true and we look forward to this special occasion. In the meantime, we must pray and enjoy the journey.

My journey begins in Sierra Leone, a small country (slightly smaller than South Carolina) in West Africa. I was born in an even smaller village by the name of Njala- Komboya and from my first introduction into this world was marred by controversy. My mother, Agnes Lebby, was a married but estranged wife who had an affair with a local college student by the name of Joseph Kinei N'Gaojia - my father. My mother's estranged husband was Teacher Tommy, as he was known through the entire town due to his educational status and diligent work habits at the local high school. Teacher Tommy was well respected in the community and he and my mother had a child, my oldest sister Regina Tommy. He was anxious to have a baby boy and when my mother became pregnant again he envisioned finally having his baby boy but tragedy struck and my mother had a miscarriage. This may have added stress into their marriage and ultimately caused them to separate indefinitely. During this separation, I was conceived and Teacher Tommy insisted that I was his son causing a child custody battle. Upon further investigation, Joseph was deemed to be my biological father.

Young Joseph was an ambitious student and he was determined to make something worthwhile out of his life. He would walk to and from school for at least five miles a day while he balanced his studies, maintaining a high-grade point average, and working on the family farm in the nearby village of Gbetima. The local resident American Peace Corp representative noticed the young college student's ferocious ability to overcome the crippling environment he was in and offered some help. My father had lost his father to an early death and now my father was designated as the bread winner. My father's cousin, Morie Goba, had recently moved to the United States and he was planning to send for my father as well. With the help of the Peace Corp, my father traveled to New York in the borough of Brooklyn before I was a year old.

Joseph's mother, Sallie N'Gaojia, a strict disciplinarian and orthodox Muslim, took custody of me due to my mother having my sister to take care of and trying to get back on her feet after divorce. As soon as I arrived at my new destination, I suffered a near-death experience stemming from a devastating infection of chicken pox. I was told I was bedridden for weeks and incapacitated. We lived in Bo, one of the major cities in Sierra

Leone. Bo was more of a commercial and urban economically driven city. I attended the catholic school which is the tradition there; all schools are ordained by the Catholic Church because of British principles the country adopted during British reign. As far as school, I attended when I could. I played hooky often. I would hang at the bus terminal where all the vehicles that traveled to and from the small villages parked daily. I roamed the area in hopes of begging for money for food, or to go back to the village to see my mother or maybe even see someone who knew me or my mother. I must have been five years old by now but five years old in Sierra Leone is a large difference to being five years old in America. I was well ahead of my years, I basically wore the same clothes every day and I barely had any shoes. I knew how to hustle. I could sell anything to anyone if I had it to sell. I was a street-wise kid wandering around the city.

My grandmother worked at the market selling knick-knacks and if she didn't make any sales that day we barely ate. I learned how to survive by begging, stealing, and at times eating out of trash cans. My grandmother was a strong authority figure, a woman that is not to be played with but I was a hard head that wanted to do things my way. I yearned for a touch from my mother. We would go to the mosque to pray our daily prayers and although my grandmother was stern, she loved me so much. I never even considered the absence of my father. She worked hard to provide what she could for me. We were extremely impoverished. I slept on the ground, just the red clay ground on a straw woven mat below my grandmother who slept on a make-shift bed stuffed with hay infected with bed bugs. To make matters worse, Nansu, my female cousin, came to live with us and she too slept next to me on that small mat. I always say to this day, no one can ever tell me about poverty. My grandmother and I never knew that my father was sending money every month from America because family members that would receive the letters never said anything. I eventually ran away to go stay with my mother in the village but that stay was short lived because my father sent for me to join him in America.

At this moment, I was eight years old and I was transported to the capital city of Freetown for me to complete all my paperwork for my trip. I remained in Freetown for a year at my uncle Patrick's house and a month after my ninth birthday I arrived in New York. I can recall all the times I spent roaming around Sierra Leone taking refuge in abandon cars. I often pray to God to change my life. I would watch the planes fly by and fantasize about being on them. Suddenly, my prayers were answered. I boarded that plane and came to America. Along with my new residence came an angel in the presence of my new mother, Lula N'Gaojia, my father's wife. She invited me into their home with a warm open heart and I called her "Mommy" from day one. I would spend most of my time in Brooklyn, New York but I attended school in Newark, New Jersey. The kids were not friendly at all; they chased me home, ridiculed me, and bullied me for not being able to speak English fluently. I was made fun of daily but Mommy always made me feel better. I eventually learned how to fight and I also perfected my language deficiency. This new environment exposed me to violence I had never witnessed in my life including drugs, weapons, and all types of corrupt lifestyles that are synonymous with the urban community. I found myself fully emerged into my new reality. I escaped gun fights, gang intimidations, and the rampant crack epidemic in my neighborhood. I learned how to fight so good that I became a boxer, a football player, and a body builder.

After high school, I attended college for a few months then I decided to go into the Army. During my 21 years of service, I deployed to Bosnia, Kuwait, Iraq for two tours, and Afghanistan. I was stationed in various countries including Germany, Korea, and Hungary. In Iraq, we experienced several artillery fires and IED attacks; I lost lots of great friends. I always wondered why God kept saving my life in these instances. There was one time that I was stabbed eighteen times all over my upper torso, even puncturing my lungs. That incident put me in a coma for three days. When I woke, Mommy was by my bedside in Germany holding my hand. A few years later, I was shot in my chest by a shot-gun that almost shattered my chest cavity. During these tragedies, I experienced two divorces that emptied out my bank accounts. And finally, in July 2010 during a routine mission in Afghanistan, we experienced a rocket attack and fortunately no one was injured but when we returned to the base my body experienced a strange medical disorder. I began to vomit relentlessly. The temperature of the fluids was so hot that you can feel the heat emanating off the ground. The pain was severe enough that the doctors would continuously pump my body with morphine. I was rushed into emergency surgery in Bahrain, Afghanistan, where they cut open my stomach, flushed all my organs, and removed any debris blocking my major bodily functions. I was not able to perform any basic human activities. After surgery, I was airlifted to Lanstudl, Germany, to recover. I lost several of my abilities such as walking properly and other personal issues. Fast forward a few years later, I lost my biological mother, Agnes, whom I have not seen since I was eight years old. Then the angel that has been by side all these years left me as well, November 8, 2013, I lost my mother Lula. Again, I'm asking God what is it that you have in store for me? Why so much pain?

I have taken my energy and pinpointed my love and talents towards acting since my departure from the military. Performing has been something I fell in love with at 11 years old. There is something about being on stage, filming a show, or movie that brings me pure joy. I always told my mother that one day I was going to become a big star and she always assured me that I have the potential to become whatever I wanted to be. My ambition is to be one of the best actors of all times. To cement that dream and bring it to reality I went back to college and graduated with a theatre degree. I don't want to be famous for the sake of fame and money but to use my position to bring exposure to Sierra

Leone. I want to help people worldwide but I want to start with my birthplace. I want to open hospitals in Agnes's name, colleges after Lula's name, and programs for people less fortunate in honor of Joseph and Sallie. I want their legacies solidified for eternity because I want the world to know that they gave life to a genius and no matter how rough the journey was I appreciate them and their selfless contributions. These days, I feel like all I have left is my acting. It is my true passion and my therapy. I don't know how I am going to get to that top spot that I am aiming for but again I didn't even know how I was going to get to America but here I am… I can't wait to take camera crews to my village so I can show the world where I come from. And to let people know that God can open all doors no matter where you are, if you believe in Him, and work hard, you can achieve anything.

Kineh Sam N'Gaojia is a native of Sierra Leone, West Africa. An actor, model, and writer, Kineh moved to the Unites States, spending his early yes in New York and New Jersey. He enlisted in the U.S. Army and served until retiring as a Captain in 2012. He is currently pursuing his acting career. He and his family reside in Charlotte, North Carolina.

2

BROKEN TO BRAND NEW

KENYA R. HENDRICKS

I can remember being molested by my stepfather like it was yesterday. Feeling him touch me and seeing him sneak in and out of my room in the middle of the night haunted me for years. It changed everything about me. I lost the ability to trust people and I became more afraid of affection. I felt like being molested robbed me of the closeness that people share. I became standoffish and unimpressed with gestures of love or admiration. Hugs or even slight touches on certain parts of my body made me buckle and the thought of an intimate relationship was unfathomable. I began to hate what I saw in the mirror. I blamed and bullied myself into believing no one will ever love someone like me. Someone who not even a father could love. My birth dad was present in the beginning but not around for a lot of my life and the man who was... was hurting me. Odds like that taught me that every man will either never be there or if he is there... he will only hurt you. Nightmares and flashbacks became a norm and with no outlet it was easy to slip into a depression. I didn't feel pretty, smart, or worthy. I retreated into my own world and created a shield so no one would ever see all the shattered pieces. Food was the only thing that made me forget and it quickly became a source of comfort. The more I ate, the more I didn't care what my life was. I was so broken.

Soon, I began to hate what I saw when I looked in the mirror. I lost myself along the way. Who was I? I'd close my eyes and wish on every star in the sky that I could miraculously turn into someone else, somebody with a smile that matched her heart. But no, I was the girl with the great personality that disguised pain, insecurity, low self-esteem, hate, self-loathing, depression, denial and shame. Never one to express my feelings to others, I chose to jot down my thoughts. Rereading them felt somewhat therapeutic. Not long after that, I began to turn the pain I had lived into poetry. It was effortless to spill my feelings and anger onto a piece of paper. I launched verbal and soul-revealing attacks against everyone and everything that I felt played a part in destroying me. It was freeing. I felt the weight of my past lift every time I wrote, and I wrote often. Poetry evolved into song and the voice I thought I'd lost years ago, finally had a sound. It felt like I had a reason to smile again… a purpose.

I remember watching *Sister Act 2*. Whoopi Goldberg's character had a line that changed my world. In one sentence, it was the complete summation of my feelings. "If you wake up and all you can think about is writing, then you're a writer." After that, I knew what I wanted to do with my life and I embraced everything about it. Those songs became stories and my stories became scripts. They all became life. What I loved about writing is that you could create anything. Words made beautiful things appear and erased even the most traumatic memories. The opportunities to rewrite the past and see one's self like you've always wanted were limitless. Love became possible and trust was imaginable through words. I even learned to forgive through writing and even though it didn't erase the haunting episodes from my past, it gave light to my future. My wounds were being repaired.

Then I lost my kin spirit one year in October. Losing my grandmother was a new tragedy for me. She was such a strong force in my life and I learned so many things from her. The most memorable thing I took away from my years with her was her faith. She loved the Lord with all that she was and she made sure that we grew up loving Him too. Not until now have I truly understood why her faith was so strong. I always wondered why she believed that everything would be all right despite the circumstances, if we just prayed and trusted the Lord. I loved God but I still worried and stressed over everything. My faith was never as strong as hers but I had it. People would always tell me that if there is even an ounce of doubt there will never be faith and it was probably the truest thing I had heard in a while but in the quest to increase my faith, I felt like the life I thought I had control of was now beginning to spiral. I never cried as much as I did in what felt like the darkest moment in my life. I had lost my way somewhere and I wanted the disappointment to end. Life had presented itself a more than powerful adversary. I had no fight left in me so ending my life to escape the pain became a contemplation but it was at that moment that God revealed himself to me.

I learned how to talk to Him and He responded by pulling me out from the despair I was in. I asked Him to reveal what my purpose was and He gave me visions. I learned the value He placed on my life and He granted me opportunities to use the gifts He had given me even as a child. When I started trusting God I didn't fear the same things. I'd learned to use my past as a catapult and not an anchor. Looking back and knowing what I know now, maybe God gave me that assignment. Maybe He chose me to live in that moment so I can become this woman. Maybe when I felt like I was alone, He was there all along. All the hurt turned into sandpaper and my journey was made smooth, simply because I trusted God. I believe that God has designed me for great things and I wake up each day with anticipation of how He will use me. When I ask Him to reveal my purpose, He teaches me more about myself, always preparing me for greater. I feel brand new.

Kenya R. Hendricks, founder of M'Rald Chyld Entertainment, is an accomplished writer, producer and philanthropist. A Detroit native, Hendricks caught the entertainment bug at an early age when she fell in love with poetry. It quickly evolved into songwriting and writing commercials, which led to storyboarding ideas for products. Before long, she was developing ideas for sitcoms, stage plays and now film. As a writer, she has penned dozens of stage play, television and movie scripts on topics ranging from animated children series to horror to romantic comedies. Her diverse background and ability to tell a story has made her a sought-after partner on writing projects.

3

FROM PAIN TO PURPOSE

L.A. LEWIS

"After reviewing all the statements and conducting countless interviews, we have no choice but to let you go." Monique Watson, Madison County School District's Human Resources Director, announced.

Coach Jared Carter sat across from Mrs. Watson and the other members of the board assigned to decide his fate as head coach of King High School. Coach Carter shook his head, unable to believe this was happening to him, after all the hard work and sacrifice he'd put into making the team what they are today. The school had received nothing but negative attention until Coach Carter signed on as the head football coach. Everyone had a healthy fear of Coach Carter. They knew he gave nothing but the best and expected the same in return. Next week they would've played in their first championship game after an undefeated season.

"Is there anything else you'd like to say?" Mrs. Watson asked.

Coach Carter looked into the eyes of each person before he spoke. "What can I say? I've pleaded my innocence. I've brought my pastor and my neighbors in to speak on my character, but none of that was enough." He'd fought and lost this battle.

The drive to his suburban home in downtown Varnado was one of the most difficult ones he'd ever made. He'd assured his wife, Darlene, and their children that everything would be fine. He was confident nothing would come of those accusations.

Instead of going straight home, Coach pulled into the empty park down the street from his house. He needed time to let it all soak in. Coach turned the radio down but left the engine running. The weather was unseasonably hot for October, but that's typical Louisiana weather.

He took a deep breath, then did what he'd heard his wife doing many times as he stood outside the bathroom door. He prayed.

"Lord, you and I both know this isn't fair. The things they said about me… about my family. Everyone in Varnado now sees me as a coach who cheats to win, who allows players who are failing in school to play on my team. They're talking about me like a dog, and there's nothing I can do to stop it. But you can? Why are you allowing this? Darlene and I prayed together before I accepted this position, and we felt you were leading us here? And for what? To go through all this?" Coach banged his fist against the steering wheel before placing his hands over his face and did what he dared not do in front of his wife and children... he cried.

In the silence of the car, after he'd cried all he could, he heard a faint voice saying, "I'm here." Coach looked around. He was still alone. He knew he wasn't going crazy... or was he?

He dried his eyes and checked himself in the mirror. He made sure before he left that he looked like the soldier his wife knew him to be.

*****

"Still nothing?" Darlene wrapped her arms around coach's neck.

He sat on the barstool with his laptop opened looking for a position that would be a good move for his family. "Nothing." He closed the laptop. "It's been seven months. If I don't find something before August, then we're stuck here for another year. I don't like the idea of moving the girls during the school year."

Darlene sat on the stool next to her husband. She placed her hand on top of his. "We'll do whatever we need to do. If God opens the door, no matter when it happens, we're walking through it. Football isn't just your passion; it's your gift. The impact you have on those players is life changing. So, stop trying to walk out of your purpose and start looking for coaching positions." She lightly elbowed his arm.

Her words sounded nice, but he saw the fear through her faint smile. Things were getting tight financially. They had to cut back tremendously to keep the house. They both knew they wouldn't be able to live off one income for long.

"I better get dinner started." Darlene walked around to the refrigerator.

Coach watched his wife moving around their gourmet kitchen that she loved so much. He felt a heavy sense of sadness thinking about taking all of this away from her. They'd struggled in the past, but this time they had two teenage daughters depending on them.

"What's that look about?" Darlene's eyes narrowed as she looked at him.

"What look?" Coach closed the distance between them and pulled his wife close. Their money was short, but the love they shared for each other was never ending.

"You were looking at me all strange." She tilted her head and awaited his response.

After all these years, all he saw when he looked at her was the beautiful sophomore he fell in love with at Tulane University.

"Just thinking about how much I love you." He playfully patted her behind. "What's that?" He felt something in her back pocket.

Her eyes widened. “Oh! I forgot to tell you. I ran into an old friend today. Well, more like your old friend.” She smiled as she reached into her pocket and pulled out the piece of paper.

“Felton Morrison? I haven’t heard from him in years. Where’d you see him?”

The sizzle of the ground meat caused Darlene to turn her attention back to the stove. “At the athletic conference.”

Darlene, like her husband, was a diehard athlete, so it was no surprise when she accepted the position as the lady’s basketball coach in a neighboring parish.

“What’s he up to now?” Coach leaned against the counter by the stove.

“We didn’t get a chance to talk much. He was speaking in another session. I saw him during our five-minute break. He hurried and wrote his number down and asked me to give it to you.”

Coach gazed at the number.

“So, are you going to use it or just stare at it?” Darlene joked as she poured spaghetti sauce over the meat.

“I don’t know.” He placed the paper on the counter. “I’m not in the mood to hear about him and all his success.”

Darlene placed her hand on her hip and gave him the momma look she gave the girls when they were doing or saying something that didn't meet her approval.

"Don't look at me like that."

"Call him." She reached up and kissed his lips before walking out of the kitchen.

Coach shook his head. She was right.

*****

Hours passed before Coach came out of his office. Darlene was relaxed in the recliner watching television.

"Your plate's in the microwave," she said never taking her eyes off the big screen on the wall.

Coach stood in front of her, blocking her view from whatever had her full attention.

Darlene's eyes narrowed. "What's that smile about?"

"I just got off the phone with Felton." Coach couldn't believe what he was about to say.

"And?" Darlene's eyes grew wide.

"He wanted to know if I'd been in touch with Mark Peters. I told him I hadn't heard from him in years. Not since his knee injury."

"The injury that ended his career." Darlene shook her head slowly.

"Yeah, he disconnected from everyone after that."

Coach sat on the sofa next to his wife.

"You spent all that time talking about Mark?" Darlene asked.

"No, but here's the part that's going to blow your mind."

Darlene sat up straighter.

"Felton just bought the Houston Texans," coach announced.

Darlene's eyes stretched even wider. "That's impressive, but why the Texans?"

"Opportunity." Coach shrugged. "That's all he said."

"Did he offer you a position?" Darlene asked biting her finger.

"He wanted to offer Mark the position as head coach."

Darlene's lip dropped. "Oh."

"But, he said he really wanted me. The only reason he didn't bother asking was because he'd heard about all the work I was doing here, and he didn't want to disrupt that."

Darlene's hands flew over her mouth. "Are you serious?"

"I'm so serious."

"You told him you're available, right?" Darlene leaned towards him.

"Of course."

Darlene jumped up and started dancing around the room. “We’re moving to Houston.” She started singing.

“We still have a lot to discuss, but it looks that way.” Coach joined his wife in a victory dance.

“What’s going on in here?” Both their daughters stood on the stairs grimacing towards them.

“Blessings are going on,” Darlene said waving the girls over to join them.

****

“Touchdown Texans!” The announcer shouted. “The Houston Texans have just won their first Super Bowl folks!”

The icy water dumped on his head only electrified the feeling Coach Carter felt on the inside. Instead of immediately running on the field with everyone else, Coach stood off to the side, looked up, and simply said “thank you.”

Bestselling Author, **L.A. Lewis** has published three novels which include Dirty Little Secrets, Dirty Little Secrets II: Expect the Unexpected, and Double Down and Dirty. A daily devotional, The Gift of An Abundant Life, and two motivational books, P.W.I.T: Phenomenal Woman In Training, and Why Not Me? A Guide to Your Success. L.A.’s a member of M-LAS, a writing support group.

Together, they've published a reference book titled, Baring it All: The Ins and Outs of Publishing. She's also a writing coach and motivational speaker. L.A. says her daily goal is to live life on purpose.

4

MY JOURNEY OF BECOMING A FAITH WALKER

JOYCE WHITE

We are all born with a purpose. Many people are not aware of this and therefore go through life not knowing why they were created. But in 1 Peter 4:10-11, it states that each of you should use whatever gift you have received to serve others, as faithful stewards of God's grace in its various forms. In verse 11, it states if anyone speaks, they should do so as one who speaks the very words of God. If anyone serves, they should do so with the strength God provides, so that in all things God may be praised through Jesus Christ.

So, everything that happens in your life is to help you discover your purpose and then once you discover your purpose, you should take the necessary steps to fulfill that purpose. Allow me to share with you how I discovered my purpose and became known as the Faith Walker.

Growing up, I was always a talker and loved to perform. When it came to taking pictures, if I saw a camera I would make sure I was in the picture. I never realized that it would eventually lead me to the career of being an entertainer. When I was in high school, I thought I wanted to be an interior designer because I loved colors and decorating. But after I graduated from high school and started attending The Art Institute of Atlanta, I struggled with learning how to draft so I gave up the idea of being an interior designer and started pursuing a degree in Business Management since I was good with office administration. I was not able to complete my degree in Business Management because I became pregnant and needed to work to provide for my daughter. But I was able to find employment with BellSouth Mobility for 13 years. I worked many positions from accounts payable, real estate administrator and customer financial services rep. While employed with BellSouth Mobility, I went back to school and received a paralegal certificate from the National Center for Paralegals. Once the company merged with another telecommunications company and told us that our jobs were being moved out of state, I started looking for a paralegal position and ended up finding a job as a conflicts analyst with a large law firm. It was while I was working there that I started moving toward my purpose.

The church I had been attending in Austell, Georgia, needed towns people for their Easter production. My friend Linda convinced me to participate and that is when I the acting bug bite me. At first, I was a towns person shouting, 'Crucify Jesus!' and then the next year I obtained a speaking part. One year, the church put on a Christmas production and I played a boss. After the play, a church member pulled me to the side and said that I should take my talent outside the church. When he told me that, something clicked inside of me so I found an acting school and started looking for projects to get involved in. I found independent films and local stage productions to help build my resume. As I got involved in projects, I discovered that I loved being on set and was not bothered by the long hours and other tedious processes involved in film and stage productions. This is how I learned that acting was my passion and one of my God-given talents.

Know that while you are pursuing your purpose it will be filled with ups and downs. One of the downs I experienced was trying to balance acting with working a full-time job. But I did not let that stop me. In 2008, I had the opportunity to audition for Tyler Perry to be a photo double for Alfre Woodard in the film *The Family that Preys*. Although I was not selected, I knew that was a sign for me to take steps to leave my full-time job and pursue acting full time. So, I found a part-time job working at the World of Coca Cola so I could pursue acting full time. After working for the World of Coca Cola for three years part time, I had to go back to working a full-time job to pay my bills and keep a roof over my head. So, with the help of a temp agency, I obtained employment with a company called nCourt doing administrative work. Meanwhile I was still finding ways to be involved in acting projects and continue working in my purpose of being an entertainer.

In 2013, I started on my journey of being known as a Faith Walker. I believe it was in July when I saw a posting on Facebook that an internet radio station, the Survival Radio Network was starting a Christian Network. That prompted me to start thinking that I should create a radio show that would encourage, educate and entertain. So, I reached out to Chuck Brown who created the post and told him I was interested in being a host. He helped me to come up with the name of my show which is Faith Walk with Joyce White. The scripture my show is based off is 2 Corinthians 5:7, *"For we walk by faith and not by sight."* I even reference this scripture on my business cards. I created my platform to allow people to share their message, music, and business to uplift a nation that needs inspiration. My mission in life is to help others enjoy life, find their purpose and walk in faith. My show aired on Tuesday September 10, 2013 at 7:30 pm. Three years later and I have been given the opportunity to co-host on two other internet radio networks, She-Praise Magazine Radio and Late Night with Jerry Royce Live on Positive Power

Christian Radio. This is what happens when you follow the plan and purpose God has for your life.

I want to encourage you to pray and ask God to help you find your purpose. Once you find your purpose, do not be afraid to dive in and start operating in your gifts. If you are not sure what your gifts are, there is a test that you can take online that will show you what they are. I took the test and discovered that I have the gift of encouraging, helps and teaching. This explained why I love to volunteer and give back to those that need assistance. I have a heart for children and volunteered as a CASA (Court Appointed Special Advocate) for Douglas County for five years and this year got involved with a program called Diamond in the Rough. Where I help mentor girls between the ages of 2-6. We call them GEMS. I highly recommend that you find an organization to get involved with. It may help you discover your purpose.

Sometimes God will use people to help you become clear on what your purpose is. In fact, he used a friend of mine to help me know for sure what my purpose is. Her name is Minister Ebony Lockhart and she created a meet up group called Discovering Your Inner Royalty which once I saw the title I quickly signed up. We had Monday

Motivational Empowerment calls where she shared a message to help everyone with a particular situation they may be struggling with. One day, she had a conference entitled Discovering Your Identity where she shared a message that actually helped me confirm that my God-given purpose is to entertain and encourage through my acting and radio ministry. Ebony also allows people to flow in their gifts. She allows me to host the conferences now and for that I am very appreciative.

It feels so good to be able to operate in your gifts. Once you are operating in your gifts there will be opposition. It may come from your friends, co-workers and yes, even your family. But it is very important that you stay in the Word of God and remove all doubt and negative thoughts. I never would have thought in a million years that I would be known as a Faith Walker. But with God all things are possible. Through this journey called life I have been able to increase my faith, decrease my doubting and truly know what it means to be a Faith Walker.

To be a Faith Walker, you must trust God with all your heart, mind and soul and know that all things work together for those that love the Lord. You must also remember that fear and doubt are the opposite of faith. Your faith will grow more when you change your mindset and stay in a positive mode. Start by deciding every morning to be happy no matter what, and when fear, anger and doubt try to creep in, squash it with the Word of God. I pray that my story has helped you with how you can find your purpose and what steps you can take to walk in your purpose. Now is the time to live the life you have imagined. All you need to do is take a leap and God will be there to help you through it all. I wish you all a successful, meaningful and happy life!

Joyce White is a radio personality, actor, model, public speaker and voice talent. She co-wrote in the book entitled, *Let Me Testify*, a book about testimonies from the hosts of the Survival Radio Christian Network. Her chapter dealt with Love Not Hurting which is her personal testimony. Joyce's motto in life is to Live, Laugh and Love. Her purpose is to Encourage, Educate and Entertain the World. She credits God for giving her the talents to be a blessing to others.

5

PURPOSE BIRTHED THROUGH PAIN

DR. CHRISTINA R. KIRK

I swear Monday through Friday when that alarm goes off for work I snooze it at least twice before crawling out from under my oversized, thick comforter. But not on the second and fourth Saturdays of the month. No snooze on these days. No dragging to get out of bed. No creeping to the shower waiting for the hot water to not only wake up my body but my mind.

What is so special about the second and fourth Saturdays of the month? They are Prep University (Prep U) class days. Prep U is girls mentoring and college preparatory program to some. But, to me, Prep U is the perfect collision of purpose and passion. It is the manifestation of my God-given purpose for my life. It is the true embodiment of being the person you wish you had in your childhood. Prep U for me is life, life more abundantly.

Several years ago, I crawled up on my chocolate brown leather sectional purchased only months before as a part of our interior decorating plan for our 3300-square foot custom built home and prayed to God to just let me die. Dying had to be better than the feeling of not being able to breathe that I experienced in those moments. Yes, I inhaled and exhaled as involuntary motions but the actual desire to want to take my next breath alluded me. My husband of 15 years and mate of 19 years walked away from the family and life we worked diligently to create as a solution to his hidden depression, leaving me, the person who had never lived alone; never experienced adult life solo; never a night with no one else in the home. Yes, that me. In the blink of an eye, I was a single mother of a tenacious teenage daughter, in a big empty house that was no longer a home, wanting to die.

In that moment, my life seemed void. I did not know what the void was simply that there was a void. As many do when their world is in crisis, I prayed. I prayed a lot. I screamed at God. I cried. I cried a lot. I screamed at God some more. Between the praying, screaming, and crying, God spoke. I just did not know it at the time.

When I finally decided to get off the sofa and literally took a shower, brushed my teeth, did my hair, and put something on other than sweats, I knew I had to do something to make my heart smile again. I immediately thought of what can I do with kids.

Working with kids, especially young ladies, had long been a passion of mine. I volunteered and led the largest

Girl Scout troop in my city for over 10 years. I spent time helping girls through mentoring and created opportunities for girls to work with other girls that were goal-minded. I worked with the youth at church. When I went to the grocery store, even the shyest little kid would always smile and talk to me. I just had a way of connecting to youth. It is my talent. I enjoyed my "day job" as a family law attorney but the kids always put a smile on my face.

For a few years, I played around with the idea of a program to give girls all that they need to be prepared for successful college matriculation. For me, my ex-husband provided the guidance and leadership I needed as a first-generation college student with limited educational family support. I knew there had to be others out there that longed for the choices education yields with or without the engagement of a relationship. In addition, as I learned to navigate the educational world, I learned many of the most prepared and accomplished (not necessarily the most intelligent) students started their path to preparation long before senior year of high school. Forcing myself off the sofa, I researched college preparatory programs looking to see what worked but had all the components I knew were vital for girls, especially girls of color. Gradually, Prep U was born.

Working on developing a comprehensive college preparatory program for girls aided as I learned my existence was not tied to my title as a wife. The more I worked on Prep U, the greater my personal confidence grew as I sought community and faith-based partnerships. The more time I invested in others and for others benefit, the more I evolved myself. The pain that once consumed me gradually faded and anticipation about the future successes of Prep U young ladies danced in my thoughts.

Along the journey to develop Prep U, many emotions from the experiences of my own teenage years reemerged. I tell Prep U often I was a hot mess as a teenager. I hid all the pain from being helpless to the hurt of others, embarrassment for a disabled mother and incarcerated father, and self-hate for longing for as many guys as possible to show me they loved me physically. Growing up, I thought God must really hate me. As my pastor preached about how God is love and full of mercy, I knew it must not apply to me. What I did not know was that God was merely preparing me. He orchestrated each disappointment, denial, and disregard to provide me with an arsenal of life experiences to share and pour into every Prep U young lady that is not something someone else told me but what I have lived and overcome by His amazing grace.

As Prep U was born, Christina was reborn. This rebirth rooted itself in the manifestation of walking into my purpose, a purpose I never imagined for myself but now I cannot imagine not having. I now choose to breathe for myself. Knowing the importance of my purpose and how it is interconnected to the destiny of so many young girls waiting for me to empower and encourage them to walk in the greatness they have on their lives. I firmly believe God used my girls, as they are affectionately called, to save and restore my life giving me a new life - one of divine pain turned to purpose.

The fulfillment I receive from every text message, call, Facebook post, Instagram shout out, or tweet cannot be measured. Each encounter with my girls fills the void I once felt. Each success of my girls, no matter how grand or small, is a smile on my face and whisper to God for allowing me the opportunity to be a part of their lives. I know who is dating whom and what friend is being petty or throwing shade but I also know who is hurting because a parent is ill and who has been scarred from situations that no little girl should experience. Intricately, my new life is woven with threads from each of my girls. The tapestry is elegantly designed so each girl feels her thread is quintessential. However, I know they are jointly and severally labyrinthine aspects of the woman I am today.

The true demonstration of this thing called purpose is peace. Walking in my purpose brought a peace to my life when all else around me was chaos. Focusing on my purpose removed space and time for focus on the uncertainties and anxieties of my post-divorce future. This peace did not come from any external stimuli. It is peace from that place just beyond my heart, my soul. For me, Prep U is a soul-stirring opportunity to serve God by serving His daughters, creating an internal peace that passes all understanding. Just when everyone, including me, thought my life ended, the peace that comes with my purpose assured me otherwise.

So, every second and fourth Saturday, I look around the house to make sure I grabbed everything I need for the day from copies of worksheets, ACT prep manuals, study guides, and even lunch for my girls. Gladly out the door, I go. Sure, sleeping in would be great. After all, I have very long weeks of balancing courtroom and classroom time. Nonetheless, I jump in the car and head to Prep University oftentimes picking up girls along the way. Prep U is the place where my passion meets my purpose, all birthed from great pain.

I never thought of pain with a positive connotation. I just could not wrap my mind around how when something hurts so bad, you no longer want to even breathe. It could turn out to be an opportunity to walk in your true purpose for your life. Yet, for me, my pain birthed my purpose. So, the next time you feel like you do not want to take that next breath, inhale the pain and exhale your purpose.

Christina R. Kirk is a woman after God's heart. After dropping out of high school, Christina earned a Bachelor's of Arts from historic Fisk University and Juris Doctorate from University of Tulsa, School of Law. Christina currently teaches and practices family law. She is also Municipal Court Judge for the City of Langston, Oklahoma. Christina's dedication to the youth is immeasurable. She has received several community service and leadership awards. She speaks at schools encouraging women about the importance of education. In dedication to her mentor, Dr. Olgesby –Pitts, Christina founded Prep U in 2009 to empower and support young ladies to a life of good success. In 2013, Christina honored her mentor and shared her story of inspiration and overcoming obstacles on the Steve Harvey Show. Christina is the proud mother of, Déja Kirk. In her spare time, she loves to travel and shop.

6

THE VOICE OF PURPOSE

ARLENE MCGUIRE

When I hear the word purpose, of course I know the meaning.

Purpose is:

1. The Reason why something is done.

2. The Determination to do or achieve something.

3. The Aim or Goal of a person.

But today the word takes on a different meaning new meaning than what I was made to believe growing up as a child from Jamaica, West Indies, and feeling my way through Harlem, New York. Without a doubt, I was clear that my purpose was to be a good wife and mother. That's what my mother drilled in me. There was nothing else for a small child from a poor country to do or be. In the 1960s and 70s in Harlem, I didn't understand all that was happening in the news and around me. I walked streets paved with torment and struggle as well as bloodshed. Yet, I was spared those very strong experiences.

Not only was I sheltered from a lot of negative experiences, I felt that I missed out on a lot of self-discovery because I was being molded to pursue the purpose that my parents wanted for me. I didn't know that I could pursue my purpose for myself.

Early on, I began writing out of feelings and became curious about my voice. I had a small radio in my room and before going to sleep at night I would use that radio to teach myself how to speak as New Yorkers or Americans in general. I had a great deal of difficulty in school with my very distinct accent. So, I would listen to a DJ named Cousin Brucie and I tried to adopt his speed and chopped speech. There, it all began, the dream of voice. Those nights of repeating what Cousin Brucie said helped a lot. In time, my native accent diminished and I was discovering another distinctive voice.

So, a new purpose was being birthed very quietly in the darkness of my tiny room. I had no idea what I was talking about or thinking. At that age, I didn't even know how my voice sounded or what I could do with it. But for some reason I was intrigued.

No one was teaching black kids anything about being a voiceover artist. We were taught to get a vocation or a civil service job. In my community, there wasn't even talk of being a doctor or lawyer. But we hear about being a hair dresser or seamstress in a factory. Becoming a secretary was a lofty goal for some. Even with those few options, my success would be judged by how well I did my job as a mother and wife.

I eventually had three children and failed marriages and tried my hardest to fulfill the purpose for my life set by others including my mother. I failed miserably. I brought shame and disgrace upon every member of my family. Those years were very painful for me. I don't know how I made it through. As I tried to gain everything for others, I lost myself. I didn't have an identity outside of being a mother and wife.

At that point, I saw absolutely no purpose to my life. I was a colossal failure and there would be no one to save me. Being a good wife and mother was no longer what I saw as the ideal life. That purpose-driven life had sent me into a nightmare spiral. So, the pain of writing began again. I do mean pain. I poured out my soul into the pages and because I had very few friends, I sought absolution through my words to Gods ears.

I had hoped to have a time when I would have a voice and purpose that centered around me and not my kids and husband. I see myself using it to provide the feeling that my voice gives to listeners. It is not something I can create. It is simply there and I had to come to terms with what the sound I produce does.

I went through a phase of defining and redefining my purpose and deciding how to go about achieving it so late in life. It was a daunting task. The feeling of failure followed me around like a dark cloud. I felt like I was closer to death than to fulfilling my purpose and living my dreams.

I can recall all the famous black stars that I saw as a youngster at the club down the street from where I lived. The greats walked on my street and in some way, I knew they were paving the way for me and so many others in Harlem. But to me, I felt the doors kept closing throughout my life. I kept dreaming that someday I would be discovered.

In 1988, I started my voiceover journey. I enrolled in classes for voiceover work. I spent time and money actively pursuing it. You can't just see it and think it's going to jump in your lap. It can but it doesn't usually happen that way. Take the journey to discover what you have and how to make it happen so that when opportunity arises you're at your best.

The one element that I felt was missing is that one person who had the key to put in, turn and let me out or in. I've paid my dues. I wasted a lot of money and time trying to figure it out. I needed someone to say that black voices were excluded from the industry in my youth. I didn't need to spend money to do what I do but I didn't have the key for the lock.

When it started to change and people were amenable to listen to black voices, there were more opportunities. In 2016, it came to fruition for me. I started helping in a hospice and sat and talked to people and made them feel better. Vertikal Reading Room, a podcast via free app where I read 30-minute segments of a book, does the same thing. I want to go to the VA Hospital and read for people. I want to record books. Maybe it's not about the fame and fortune like I used to think. I want my voice to bring joy to people. The determination was to continue to study. The goal *was* to be well known but now it's to reach out to people who might never know me. I just want to bring joy with my voice. Finally, I can say to someone… don't give up. I kept going. I never stopped.

Arlene McGuire grew up in Harlem, New York, with my family who all came to the US from Jamaica, West Indies. As a young person, she loved words, including reading and writing essays, which allowed her mind to take flights of fancy and sharing for others to enjoy. In addition to her dream of being a writer, Arlene desired to be a voiceover artist, which she achieved as a podcast narrator in the Vertikal Reading Room. She is currently writing her second book, which is scheduled to be released soon. In her spare time, Arlene enjoys painting and spending time with her grandchildren. She and her husband reside in the Atlanta area.

7

MY PATH TO PURPOSE

APRIL WHEELER

Finding my purpose in life was a very difficult and tedious process. I didn't realize that it included every emotional, material, natural, physical and psychological aspect in life. My road is no different from anyone else's because there is nothing new under the sun. Everyone has trials and tribulations but it was what I did with my life that changed the path that could have led me to destruction. I decided to purposely seek and follow my own guidelines to a different purpose. The steps to finding my road to purpose were simple. I had to decide where I wanted my life to go, live and let go, find peace and send out positive vibes, learn and experience while building up my confidence, and surround myself with people who encouraged me to push a little harder to do different things.

I searched for my purpose when I was at one of my low points in life. The world I was in sounded loud and drawn out, I felt alone like my mind and heart were so overworked that it was empty and just running on air. I asked why me on several occasions until one day why not became the question. This question was the motivational force to finding out where my life was going and how to fulfill my purpose. I decided to change and live in that change. I had to build myself for my children because they were my biggest driving force to set my path. I needed to make them safe in all aspects of life because it was tough trying to explain the things that were going on around them. It was my job to lead them to their purpose.

It was imperative to figure out what was holding me hostage. I felt certain people caused chaos and confusion in my life. My emotions would always get the best of me. I created a list of all the things I wanted to change. I listed them as headaches, heartaches, and rashes. My headaches with life affected my brain. My head was clouded and I often made the wrong life-changing decisions. My heartaches with life left me broken and afraid to let anyone in. My rashes were irritations that made my skin crawl but would disappear with time. I dealt with my heartache first. I had to let go of my woe is me state and finalize my emotions for people, places and things. There were three things I asked myself. Can I do without this heartache/headache in my life? Does this heartache help me though my life from the heart or with ill intent? Can I love this heartache or interact gracefully with this heartache from a distance? If the answer was no to any of those questions I would slowly start to faze them out accordingly. I was always courteous but didn't involve myself in reckless behavior anymore. It saved me from unnecessary disasters that didn't serve the path to my purpose and letting go. My purpose path was in full effect. I felt so much better when I let go. It took time to realize that everything leaves road signs to a person's purpose.

Peace was the most precious word for my path, its freedom from disturbance. Peace is quiet. I love peace like a queen size blanket of soft coated chocolate. Everything I did I had to resemble peace so when I slept at night, it would be a peaceful sleep. How awful would it be if I acted out of peace and destruction fell into my kids' lives? Finding time for me played a crucial part to my path. I had a very busy schedule so I picked a couple of hours a day for me to work on the goals I set for myself from the inside out.

I would ask myself a lot of questions and started searching for the answers on how to create my path to purpose. I took the time to learn something new every day. I researched the word love one night. Love is an intense feeling of deep affection. I got into the type of love one can show. There was Eros, a passionate love; Philia, a friendship shared with good will; Storge, the love between family members; Agape, a universal love for strangers, nature or God; Ludus, a playful uncommitted love/the love of fun; Pragma, the call to duty of love; and Philautia, the love of self. I let these terms sink in and applied them to everyday life accordingly. Sometimes I found it was hard to love but, I did it anyway. Showing love was a lot easier than hating someone.

I found myself concentrated on Ludus Love, the love for fun and the word experience stuck out. Everyone loves to have fun even if they don't admit it. I was not in the position to experience life. I was a home body. I went to work, school and home. I did not have an identity and was not excited about life anymore. I wanted to learn new things, become my own person, and be happy. I was not enjoying all the opportunities that were lying at my feet. My learning experience opened my eyes to awesome things and new possibilities. I found new interests and build up my confidence even more. I was doing things I had never done before. I noticed I felt the same way after getting off a rollercoaster, when I took a road trip and doing or receiving something special.

It was good for me to push my limits and see where my adventures would take me while being safe. I vowed to be confident and happy in any situation because I never know when I will have to stand in confidence. It took years and hard work to build my path and I still had clean up to do. People noticed how happy I was. Eventually, it would spill over into their lives. I learned some very good lessons from some of them. At the least, my purpose was to give some individuals a fun day's worth of pay.

I felt the need to be around friends and family that would encourage me to try new things. This was a big help to create my path. It left me with great memories that shadowed the hectic days. I was going though. I found that people were put in my path sometimes just for clarification of life from my perspective. I carefully picked and chose battles so I could keep all my love intact. It was not for me to pick sides but for me to be real with my feelings and not to harm others because of my emotions. I was still available to dish out love with more confidence that led me to my purpose. I continued to keep happiness around me and sent out positive vibes as often as I could. I was determined to not let anything divert my path.

It was the tiniest things that would give me clarification that I was on the right path. I ended up in right place-right time situations where people were encouraged by my smile or the words of encouragement I would offer. It would happen so much I could do nothing but stand back and look at God in awe.

Displaying a positive attitude played a major role because it put some great people on my path. Life showed me that along with mercy, my purpose renews every day. Some may not reach their full purpose until they are on their death bed. I hope to strengthen you to find and stay on your path. People make physical commitments all the time but if you do not put your soul into it, you can be lost forever on the same road. Always seize the opportunities to act on fulfilling your purpose. Your purpose for the time may have already been fulfilled but did you pick up your next assignment?

Deciding where I wanted my life to go was the most important step. It was my foundation to build a path. I lived and let go and it kept me energized through this process. Sending positive vibes into the atmosphere affected everyone around me, making life more enjoyable. I had the chance to keep experiencing and learning life and surrounding myself with people who offered encouragement. I learned that it was okay to be scared because it was a part of living. Once you are on the road to your purpose, all the things that once haunted you will feel like yesterday's news.

April Wheeler is a native from Pittsburgh, PA who is family oriented. She has worked and supported many church organizations and start out businesses in her area while going to get her associates for Business Management. April continues to inspire those around her to practice better living and to believe that anything is possible.

8

PURPOSE

SONI WILKERSON BASKERVILLE

Being sexually and mentally abused as a child was rough. Reports show 1 out of 4 women have been sexually abused and 1 out of 6 boys are as equally abused. Most cases go unreported. We all have a purpose and sometimes until we find ourselves, we may go through unnecessary hurt and pain. From birth, some of us were taught that life is a struggle and that you must endure ups and downs to get happiness out of life. God wouldn't put more on you than you can handle.

Once we realize the power within us and understand that you create your life and destiny, that's when you begin to live in life's purpose. God made us in His image and gave us dominion over the earth. We must know and believe that life and death is in the power of the tongue. Think about it! I'm speaking from my own personal experiences to bring hope and truth. We must learn to shift our awareness, our minds, and stop thinking about past hurts and pains.

Thinking about the things in our lives that we don't want may seem hard at first. I challenge you to write down the positive things in life. Write down what you love, what you're thankful for and what you want. I kid you not, you will feel good and the law of attraction will manifest in your life. When we focus on things such as bills, money and betrayal, it almost always shows up in our lives. YOU are in control of your life. The moment you allow a negative thought in your mind, know that you have the power to shift your awareness and think of something wonderful.

It wasn't until I changed my way of thinking and from being a negative person, that I saw growth or change in my marriage, children or in me. Now, I'm learning to be in tune with the universe/God. It can make a mood change much easier. I realized that I am in control of my feelings. No one can make me mad. If I get upset, it's because I allowed it to happen.

With all the negative things in the world we face daily, it may be hard to feel joy. Peace. I can do it and so can you. I am a person that was broken many times in life. At times, I felt as if I didn't want to live anymore. Some of you might feel that this is the easy way out as well. But I want to encourage you to live. You must realize that you can change your situation by changing your thoughts that will change your feelings. Once you feel better, you'll want to do good deeds and good will come back to you. It's imperative to take time for yourself and meditate to clear your mind. It always goes back to changing your thoughts.

I could still be bitter and angry at my mom, angry at my husband for having children outside our marriage, and even angry at myself for having an affair as well. I could be upset with my children for all the things they do to push my buttons and upset at friends and family that walked out my life. I no longer deal with things the same. I shifted my awareness and now I realize I was always a good person. I've had plenty people for whom I sheltered, given money and cooked. But I was such a negative person who never completed much. I gained some accomplishments but I wasn't living my purpose! I didn't understand what I did to make people walk out of my life. I didn't feel it was because I was evil, mean or boring. It was my negativity attracting other negative people.

Look at the people you're around and the type of energy you surround yourself with. Really look! We must guard ourselves even if it means removing negative energy from life. Sometimes you may feel lonely but you can do it. The positive energy you're giving and your new glow will attract like-minded people. Stop making excuses for why things won't work. If you are waiting on things to be perfect in life, you might be waiting forever. God's not going coming out of heaven to say "My child, do this" or "My child, do that". His spirit lives in us and we have intuitions. He has equipped us with the knowledge to do all things.

Make sure you feed your mind with positive, educational, motivational and inspirational things. Take time to be quiet and listen to yourself. Turn the radio and television off. My husband and I believe the word television stands for "tells lies to your vision". It's sad what's happening in the world. I love each person of the world, even my enemies.

My story is still being written every day. I face new challenges and ask myself, "What are you going do?" My thoughts are, "I'm going to live through it and do it with love." We can even attract money in our life. I'm still working on this but let me tell you, I read that our mind is so powerful. I wasn't sure I truly believed in the teaching. It said try attracting something as small as a cup of coffee. I was like "Ok, whatever." My dryer was making a loud noise for weeks and drove us crazy'. I banged on it and kicked it as if it was going to fix it. Well, it didn't stop that moment but later that day my daughter said, "Mom, the dryer is not making any noise." I had chills all over my body. I was happy and scared all at the same time. I command you to work in the name of Jesus. Mind blowing, right?

My next step is to attract more money. I haven't seen a big change in my financial situation because I was focused to free my mind, body and soul. I'll keep you posted on my progress. I made a vision board and on it wrote myself a check for $200,000, my desired yearly income. I'm putting that out in the universe and I'm not wondering how I'm going do it. I just know that I will achieve this goal. I will attract the right people to mentor and guide men. It's no accident that you're reading my story. I recommend that you get a mentor as well.

Once you write down what you want, ask for it. Believe! You can obtain it! Believe! Believe! Believe! I never thought that I could be delivered from my pain. I thought I would always have to struggle. I'm blessed to wake up every day and have another chance to transform my life into what I want it to be. How powerful is that?

My purpose is to reach as many people as I can with my life's story, and:

- To let people know even at your lowest point you have the power to change your situation.
- To help people have hope and know there's power within.
- To provide resources for families and help them meet their needs so we can stop having broken parents raising broken children!
- To give hope and love.
- To provide the tools needed to help drop prison rates.
- To be productive in society.
- To be ok with stepping out on faith and trying new things.

If you don't know exactly what you want right now or what your purpose is, it's ok. Experience life, try new things, live life to the fullest and enjoy every step along the way.

Soni Wilkerson Baskerville is a native of Harrisburg, Pennsylvania. She moved to Atlanta five years ago to pursue a career in acting and modeling. The 37-year-old mother of six and wife of a nine-child blended family, is a first-time writer who always dreamed of sharing her story to inspire and motivate others.

9

LIVING IN YOUR PRUPOSE

CHARRON MONAYE

On November 29, 2008, I stood in front of a judge accepting a charge that did not belong to me. I did this to honor a man that vowed to be an honest and loyal provider but failed to pay our rent for three months. Now you may be asking, "Why didn't you pay it, Charron?" My answer to that is I was unemployed and unaware. After I had our baby boy, my ex-husband begged me to quit my job and stay at home to take care of our son. He promised to handle all the bills and provide for the boys and me and I believed him. But not even a year after that promise, I stood alone in a courtroom pleading for the judge to give me 30 more days to pay the past due amount of $2,978.52 that my husband told me he had paid. After hearing the judge's decision, I owned my verdict and let out an "ugly" cry because not only did I receive a judgment against me, I did not have the $2,978.52 that I promised to pay. But I know a God that said, *"Let not your heart be troubled: ye believe in God, believe also in me."* In addition, I have a gift and a purpose that I did not fully tap into and in that moment, I thought to myself, "You are more than a conqueror. This set up can only bless you forward." It was in that storm that I realized that it was time for me to pick up pen and paper and use my gift to inspire, motivate, and prevent everyone from going through what I just endured.

When we look at purpose, we think about the reason why something exists. We question its presence, benefit, and ability to ensure that it adds value to our atmosphere, right? So, when we examine our purpose, we must also look at our “Why” and “What”. “Why do I exist?” and “What value do I contribute to myself and others?” If you can answer those two questions, you are ready to soar and live in abundance, but if you feel challenged by these questions, I am here to give you a little crash course in purpose.

Let’s go back to my day of reckoning. That moment happened because I gave my husband the power and the key to my future. Whatever he said was law because he had the benefits and income to dictate my moves. This was a recipe for a disaster. I let my guard down and believed that he would never disappoint me, but what I also did was forget that I should have planned and prepared for the what-ifs. I could have used my down time to embark on my gift as a writer and my calling to be the voice for the voiceless. So, because I obeyed my husband and dishonored who I was, I had to lose and that loss came with a hefty price. However, I found myself, my own voice, and my strength which in return opened the doors so that my purpose could be fulfilled. On October 26, 2009, I signed my first publishing deal and was preparing to release my first book entitled, "My Side of the Story", which is a book of poetry that spoke the words that many women wanted to say out loud but could only whisper in their sleep. That release signed, sealed and delivered me. I was on the road to living in my purpose. This release afforded me the opportunity to experience what "well done" sounds like.

Soon after releasing my book, I decided to elevate my writing and I wrote and co-produced the stage play, "Living your Life", that told my story of being with a man who took my voice and made me believe that living as a wife and mother was all that I was entitled to. I examined the verbal and emotional abuse, the court case, my request for a divorce, and my desire to live in my purpose. When people watched the play, there wasn't a dry eye in the theater. Afterward, all I heard from the audience was, "You told my story." Men and women alike let me know that November 29, 2008, was my gift from God. I needed a lesson and a testimony that gave God glory and showed just how marvelous his love is. I needed to feel what it felt like to lose. I needed to understand why living for me was necessary. I went from being belittled in the eyes of the law to being purposeful in the eyes of people who were tired of being tired. I set the example that adversity can only knock us down, but grace will always be one step behind to pick us up!

Since that day, I have been walking in purpose, living in abundance, and enjoying life the way God has intended solely for me. I went from having no voice to writing and publishing five books, writing and producing two stage plays, writing seven songs considered for Grammy awards, and now coaching, publishing and writing for others. I have five authors in my publishing house and have written scripts and books for some amazing people and celebrities. Not only have I discovered why I exist, I now appreciate the shift that happened in my life on November 29, 2008. It was at my lowest that God showed me just how high I could go and I don't think I am done climbing yet.

Understanding and discovering your "purpose" only works when you are ready to be honest, transparent, committed, and dedicated to the idea of YOU! I had to get so uncomfortable with the thought of depending on people that I was forced to create a life that guaranteed me success with or without someone. I had to accept and acknowledge the ugly truths about myself so that I could attain the greatness that was waiting for me. I had to stop blaming my ex-husband and everyone else that did me wrong and I had to own my part, learn from it, and proceed in change. Living in your purpose requires you to get clear about who you are and where you want to go. Living in your purpose requires you to get consistent about when you wish to pursue and who can accompany you on your journey. Living in your purpose demands prayer, love, and laughter. I can guarantee you, if you examine yourself, own your imperfections, and get comfortable knowing that the journey to purposefully living can be uncomfortable, the rewards, in the end, will rain in abundance. Trust me, there have been times when I wanted to quit and go back to the "old Charron" and curl up in my blanket and watch movies, but then I think, "Why would I give up on me when God believed in me enough to bless me?" So, for the past eight years, I get up and show up prepared to touch someone or bless someone with an opportunity that will take them from scarcity to prosperity. I live now to give others what God gave me, a second chance to get it right. Amen!

I pray that after reading this testimony, you are inspired, empowered, and motivated to walk in your purpose or level up to live in your abundance. I went from nothing to something, simply because I listened, discovered, and answered my purpose, and I want the same for you. In my last two books, "Loving the Real You" and "Stop Asking for Permission & Give Notice", I teach, testify, and provide actionable steps you can take to own your life and your greatness. If you are tired of living in circles or feel that you haven't yet tapped into your full potential, I pray that these stories, testimonies and words of wisdom get you motivated enough to take the first step so that God can take the second one for you. I hope my testimony not only gave you hope but reminded you that your setback is truly your set up for an amazing comeback. No one thought I could bounce back from that day, but God! Believe in Him and trust in You and watch the manifestation of glory! You are truly worthy of it!

History will show that **Charron Monaye** is a writer who is not afraid to pen the thoughts, feelings, and truths that many people hide out of fear. Her body of work spans over two decades to include: 5 published books, 2 produced stage plays, ghostwriter for many and the Owner/Founder of the company, "Pen Legacy". She is a woman who is devoted to assisting others reach their greatest potential by using what she has learned within her journey to help propel others towards theirs.

10
WHAT IS PURPOSE?

CHRISTIANA S.

What is purpose? To me, purpose is God. Purpose is a lasting joy that no one can take away from you. Purpose is a fulfilment of life, the ultimate thing that you were created to do and was destined to be.

When I was young, I was a bundle of love. I loved making people smile because I loved seeing others experience a sense of warmth. I also loved and was always attracted to the arts. I loved to act, dance, and sing because it was another world for me to be anyone I wanted to be. It gave me so much joy not just to perform but to share this gift with others. Performing was a sense of release, a sense of peace and I felt it was where I belonged. As I got older, I grew to love the arts even more and wanted to share love with others even more. I did not know that it was my purpose until I got older. It seemed that God reminded me that my purpose wasn't tied up in what this world had to offer. My purpose was tied up in what I was born to do, who I was born to share my gift with and the seeds I was appointed to plant in this world. As I got older and really sought God on my purpose, I found out that my love for the arts was like the shining wrapper that covers a gift… it attracts people to the gift. The gift itself was on the inside. What was my gift? Love. My purpose was to spread love and that love came from God. Thus, my purpose was wrapped up in God and I alone had the ability to share it in such a way that it pointed to God in my creative talents.

What I can say about purpose is never abandon it, never question it, and never limit it by what you have or don't have. Trust God's plan, trust God's process, and allow your joy to take over. Understand that when you have a purpose in life that IS your job! Your purpose is something that no one can take away from you because it's the one thing that God called you to be great in. Accept what you were born to do unafraid. Understand that your purpose is your ministry. When you get frustrated, take a break, rest, pray, seek God but never quit. In the end, you alone are responsible for the seeds that God wanted you to plant while you're here on this earth. Take time to explore what you are born to do. Don't let anyone take away or distract you from your purpose. There is a plan for your life and God calls it a great thing… Never be ashamed for what God called you to do. Your purpose is a part of you… it's a part of God so live it loud, bold and with joy in your heart!

A CONSUMING FIRE

I am Twisted
Meant for perfection
Sometimes wise in my own eyes
I take my own way
Only to be circled back around
From whence I came

Spiraling Upwards
Reaching above
Even though I know
I have tumbled and I have failed
Nevertheless, success has attached its name
Permanently to mine
Educating me that nothing below is worth fighting for
Greatness is a STAR yet to be conquered

I am Shaken by Loudness

"His Voice Shook the Earth"

I am consumed with His Fire
Oldness burns within my Soul
My Heart bleeds red and orange
I do not recognize who I am anymore
I had a choice; I've chosen to be better

I am Consumed with His Light
While walking in an unknown darkness
I do not strive to touch
Still, I cannot help but touch the touchless
Firing up a wick of dullness
Detaching from a position on the empty shelf
I am ignited into an atmosphere
Only to be used by the source behind my light

My solvent forms all shapes, sizes and colors

I am a Consuming Fire
Unworthy of a Beautiful Scent
I did not pick my fragrance; it was chosen for me
I light the room with a sweet aroma of Praise
I am a bouquet of Confidence, humbleness and love
My product reads "name brand"
However, I myself… am nameless
Just a voice in the wind
Until my purpose is fulfilled
Glowing from the reverence and fear
Mediator of a Covenant; I

"Shall not escape"

His Love
For I am the Light
I am flames
That shatters the darken cries

I AM A CONSUMING FIRE!!!

(Influenced by: Bishop Dale C. Bronner's Sermon: "God: A Consuming Fire")

<u>Apple Tree of Dreams</u>
<u>(The Digger (Version 2))</u>

Dig, Dig, Dig… I'm digging hard
Digging a hole for my seed to go into
Making room for a Promise
That the Almighty have bestowed upon my life

Rebellious Dirt, seeking its way downward
Quickly my iron dragon strikes against disobedience
Parting the ways for revelation
Displaying change

I dig, dig, dig… I'm digging hard
Opening the hole
Placing my golden ticket within the mist
Praying for increase
A passion birth from nakedness

Covering… covering up my piece
My seed will spring from a kiss of breath belief
I let the dirt flow back downwards
Saying a Prayer for God's deliverance

Sprinkling water for nurturance
Feeding a magnificent sun unto my worth
A source of power
A blending of nutrition

Watering my worth
My mentality develops into prospect
As my Muster seed
Sprints over loops of boundaries
Establishing roots of equality

Toxic Protectors shun insects away

Making destruction less visible
Making growth apparent
For Increase

I drizzled water
Not too little
Not too much
As my seed soars upwards
Like an Eagle in Paradise
Passion Blooms into Tall Blessings
Fruit of Rest glistens in the sun

Peacefulness, Love, Truth
Patience, Good Nature, Wisdom
Discernment, Purity, Holiness
A Tree of Life
Beautiful Pictures
Decorating the Blue Skies
As White Fluffy Rings
Capture the essence of meaning
From my little seed

Gifts breathe the life of my Grand Willow
Wonderment of Generations
Started from my little seed
Dancing now upon the reflection of the river
Products of belief started within me
Out of streams to Faith

My Apple Tree
My Digging—the watering
The maintenance of God
Paid off in the end
A Vision of success
Left as a testimony to others
Of what can become of a Total

Transparent Praise
With just a little seed of Faith

Meaning of Life

Life is full of meaning
Time and places we can't get back
Life is full of adventure
Little surprises that pass our way
Life is full of challenges
Times that make us strong
Life is full of love
It comes across our life in tiny kisses of hope

Life is full of wonderment
Captured by twinkling moments
But the best moment of all
Is when we live our life in full effort
In fullness of our "Purpose"
It's the essence of why we are born
The answer to our soul
The therapy to our hearts
The guidance of our minds
The Destiny we must live out loud

From the moment you enter the World
From the moment that you leave
God bestows a sense of Purpose into our lives
It gives us a stance of empowering the world around us
Empowering the world in us
And living bolding in confidence

Our "Purpose" is what drives us towards greatness
Our "Purpose" is what life really is all about
The smile beneath our worth and our beauty

Life is full of meaning
For nothing in this world will ever come close

To what God created you to do
So stand tall, hold your head up high
For you my dear have a job to do
Something that no one can ever take away
LIVE YOUR PURPOSE IN GOD'S WAY

Purpose

I walk among greatness
I stop the end of times
I spit truth in eras of lies
I conquer the limits that's not known to man
I am not afraid of what is before me
For I am a Solider of the most high King
What the World calls me doesn't penetrate my soul
For I know whose I am and what I was called to do
My greatness lies in God's glory
And I proudly make my mark in Life
For I have found something that is so precious to me
Than any diamond that was created
I have found my Purpose
And living my life exactly how God imaged me to
For that I walk in my own truth
Spreading Love and giving others
A sense of freedom to live their life unafraid
Living in their own Purpose in truth

Christiana S. is originally from Detroit, MI. She is a proud Alumni of *Mosaic Youth Theatre of Detroit* and a Phenomenal Lady of *Zeta Phi Beta Sorority Inc.* She always had a love for poetry that was instilled in her by her parents at a young age. As her love for writing grew, she pursued and received a Bachelor's of Arts Degree in English and Theatre from Kentucky State University. In her spare time, she is an actress, loves to dance, paint, and hang out with family and her friends. This multifaceted, cultural woman thrives on being a positive role model for other young ladies and believes that with God ALL things are possible. Christiana knows that God has a great purpose for her life and stands true to this statement from one of her poetry collections: "I AM: the Legacy of Yesterday, the Inspired of Today and the Promise of Tomorrow." She thanks all her family and friends for their wonderful support and love. She now resides in Atlanta, GA.

11

WHAT'S NEXT?

NICHO CHARISSE

The sky was clear on a warm yet not humid 78-degree day. It was a good day to go to the flea market. Usually, I bring my mom and my daughter along but today was different. I wanted to take my time. I didn't want to be disturbed. I am decorating a house as a special project. It's a large Victorian style home, built in the early 1930s. The owner having completed the actual remodel requested my help after seeing some of my earlier work. The owner suggested that I work my magic furnishing the house on a weekend while he was away. What a perfect opportunity to create with no one in my way.

I love getting to a flea market when it first opens. There is rarely anyone around. The drunks are still asleep and only true flea market lovers make the trek first thing in the morning. So far, nothing has been picked over. A flea market has many treasures. Hopefully, I can find something extraordinary before someone else has their eye on it.

While walking through, I pick up some fruits and vegetables. There are so many wonderful things to touch and explore. Along with the food, I wound up having to walk back to my truck to drop off two lamps that I found. I will need to repair them but I can make it work. When I came back from the parking lot, I realized that I had not even gotten halfway through this place and there was so much to be seen.

I've been here an hour so far and the temperature had already seemed to have gone up a few degrees. This should not have surprised me for the beginning of August. Sweat began forming and running down my back. It was a little uncomfortable. I felt like something was crawling all over me. But I pressed because I had a goal.

I came across a section where they sold used furniture. Some pieces are extremely unique. I began picking out a few items for my projects. I knew I'd have to get some assistance carrying everything to the truck or I would have to drive down to the site but that was a last resort. While standing amongst these antiques, I thought I heard someone calling my name. It's not a common name like "mom", so whomever it was would have to be calling me. The voice didn't sound familiar. I heard it again. The voice seemed to be coming from my right as if someone was standing beside me. But there was no one here except a couch. I walked around it to see if someone might be hiding behind it and playing games. I really do not have time for this, I thought.

"What are you looking for? I'm the one that called

you," a voice proclaimed.

I stood straight up. I know it is hot outside but there is no way this couch is talking to me.

"Yes, it is me trying to get your attention," the voice said.

"Who are you?"

"Wow! It's been that long? You don't remember me."

I took a closer look. The couch was red with gold stripes. The carvings on the wooden arms and feet were badly scratched. The red material had a rip across the seat. I walked to the back of it. I discovered it had been badly torn there as well. On closer inspection, I realized the material was not the original cover. The original white was still underneath. It was discolored and you could barely tell that it once was a pure cloud white with tiny pink flowers adorned with green leaves.

"I do remember you! My how you have changed."

"You're not the skinny little girl with the thick schoolboy glasses I used to know either."

I chuckled as I ran my fingers across the wood-carved

design. I remember thinking that it looked as if it was created by loving hands. This work was made by a machine.

“I would ask how you have been but that would be dumb.”

“I would agree," the voice chuckled. "Sit for a while. It’s been a long time since anyone has."

Strangely, I became a little excited as if I was reuniting with an old friend that I had not seen in a while. Yet suddenly, I was reminded that I was talking to a couch.

“Please, I insist. I may be old and my cushions are worn and torn but I have a strong frame,” it said.

I looked around to make sure no one was looking or listening to me talk to this old couch. Once I leave this place, the psych ward will be my next destination. I laughed to myself. Taking my time, I sat down slowly. I didn’t want to make the tears any larger. Plus, I was afraid of being poked by a spring.

“How did you know who I was? Are you sure that you really remember me?” I asked hesitantly.

Right before the couch began to speak, I felt the

cushions under and behind me adjust. Suddenly, sitting there became very comfortable.

“I was not in your home. You used to babysit your two little cousins while your aunt and uncle went out.”

With a surprised looked on my face, I began to look around again to see if someone was seriously playing a prank on me.

“Yes, I did.”

“Please tell me how everyone is doing?”

“My cousins are doing well. The oldest one works hard every day. He has a boyfriend and is enjoying his life.”

“Did you just say HE has a boyfriend?" The couch exclaimed.

"Well, I don’t think it really should surprise me. I remember his fascination with Patti LaBelle and he did dress like her for Halloween that one year.”

I had forgotten about that. But he is who he is and I love him even if others don’t. I continue to update the couch on the family it serviced.

“His sister has two children and handling being a

single mother well. We don't talk much. Most of our communication is Facebook and even that is more so hitting the 'Like' button."

"And your aunt? She was such a nice lady. I loved her handwriting and the things she could do with a needle and thread. Remember when she embroidered your name on a pair of jeans?"

"She passed away a few years ago."

"Oh no! Was it from the abuse? I remember the fights. Your uncle was a very harsh man."

The sweating had stopped a while ago but now a few tears had begun to fall.

"Yes, my uncle could be cruel especially when he was drinking. She actually died from cancer."

"Oh, I am so sorry. She was so young. I remember when she was pregnant and your uncle came home drunk starting a fight with her. You tried to defend her but instead he grabbed you and threw you up against a cabinet."

I felt anger coming over me and then the sweating resumed. My blood pressure must be up.

“That was a long time ago. We have all grown up. Some of us have achieved growth while others have just gotten older.”

“How about we talk about something more positive?”

I nodded in agreement while wiping tears and looking around again to see if there were people around. It just amazed me how the couch remembers some of the things that had happen.

“So,” clearing its throat, “there was a time when you weren’t babysitting your cousins. You were asked to watched the house for the weekend when they all went away.”

“Oh yeah, I remember that. Wow!”

I began to blush because I already knew what it was talking about.

“So, what happened to him?”

“He is around. I see him once in a full blue moon.”

“You mean nothing ever happened after that night?”

He was a friend and nothing more. We hung out all the time and talked on the phone. One weekend, I called him to keep me company. We sat on the couch, laughed, and watched TV like any other day that we've hung out. This day was different. We made out on the couch. Then kisses were deep and the movements were with a harmonizing rhythm. At that time, that was enough for me but I often wondered what could have happened.

"He came to my house once a few years ago, and I tried to pursue him again. He rejected me. Guess I was more attractive back in the day."

I started laughing. To think I could go back in time. The longer I sat on this couch, the more emotional I was becoming.

"Explain to me why you remember so much. It's been years since I've seen or sat on you."

"I am filled with the tears of joy, the blood of pain, the sweat of affection and the pressures of happiness. These things keep me strong and are the desire of my continued existence. You are the first person that I shared the memories of your life so that you can compare your past with your present. This may be the end for me and many that have sat on me had many new beginnings and never looked back. It's not just me, it's other furniture and the walls that absorb the lives of those we encounter."

"The place was destroyed so long ago. You may be all that is left."

There was an extremely long period of silence between us. I sat there and thought about other things that had happened we didn't even begin to touch on. I swore I could feel the couch's heartache and heard it whimper. I leaned back as if I was back in the living room long ago. I watched the sun begin to set as if I was looking at a large screen television. Didn't realize how late it had gotten and I don't think the market employees realized someone was still here.

It's been about two years since that conversation. The house that I had been working on has since been completed. I go over there sometimes because they have jobs at other homes that I do. When I'm there, I always make sure I sit on the couch. Oh yeah, when I left the flea market I took the couch with me. I restored it with new cushions and other materials. I even took it to a friend to have the wood sanded, had the carvings redesigned as much as possible and refinished.

I believe the couch and I have an understanding. We

no longer talk about the past because we both have a future.

Nicho Charisse is a first-time author who has several projects underway. She is married with two children and two grandchildren. Nicho and her family reside in Pittsburgh

FOR OTHER TITLES
FROM EX3 BOOKS
VISIT EX3BOOKS.COM